# SENIOR ADULT
## *Program Builder*
## No. 1

Resources for fellowship, inspiration, and outreach

*Compiled by* Paul M. Miller

For the most practical use of this material, it is suggested that the group using the booklet obtain at least three copies: one to be used by the director and the others to be clipped for participants. Please remember that all of the material in this publication is protected by copyright laws.



lillenas
PUBLISHING COMPANY
PO Box 419527
Kansas City, MO 64141

# *CONTENTS*

## Skits and Scripts

## Poetry for Recitation and Reflection



## Fellowship Activities

# The Man Who Did Good

*A Chancel Play*

**by Bill Bodell**

**Setting:**

The front of any church; chancel platform and first two rows of pews.

**Characters:**

NARRATOR
OLIVER HURST
MAYOR
MAYOR'S WIFE
MINISTER
OTHER PARISHIONERS

NARRATOR stands at side lecturn. MINISTER is in pulpit on other side of the chancel platform. OLIVER enters from rear of the sanctuary. He walks timidly up center aisle to the right front pew. Sits at other end of pew from center aisle. PARISHIONERS turn and watch him walk to his place.

NARRATOR: Oliver Hurst had done a good thing. Not an expensive thing, mind you. His wallet was much too thin for that. He had done *good,* though in life he had not done *well.* His old Webster's dictionary had long ago taught him the difference between the two words. Each Sunday morning, Oliver was somewhere in the congregation.

(MINISTER *searches congregation from the pulpit, finally sees him off to his left, smiles contentedly and nods.)*

NARRATOR: The minister never fully settled into his sermon until he had located the familiar graying head, its sprightly cowlick undaunted by passage of time. Each Sunday, Oliver sat in a different place.

(PARISHIONERS *turn, looking back through the congregation in search of* OLIVER. OLIVER *gets up, moves to left side, second pew.* PARISHIONERS *turn back, one by one, and see him.)*

NARRATOR: No one fully understood, and none dared ask, why OLIVER moved from place to place each week. When the sermon was very, very long . . .

(PARISHIONERS *stretch their arms above their heads and yawn.)*

NARRATOR: Or insufficiently inspiring . . .

(PARISHIONERS' *heads drop, as though asleep.)*

MINISTER *(in a voice that instantly brings them alert):* However!

NARRATOR: The congregation played their game called "Looking for Oliver." Very discreetly, of course, they sought him out. *(Points)* Halfway up on the left, one time. *(Cue: heads turn)* Back pew, way over on the right the next. *(Points. Cue: heads turn.)* The weeks went by. For a few minutes each Sunday, they thought of Oliver. As much as he could, Oliver thought of God. *(Mysteriously)* And that other thing. The good thing he had done. Six months have passed since they first began to notice Oliver. From being nobody *(peers out, holding hand above eyes),* he has become a man to watch—ever so discreetly, of course. When the service was over, no matter where he sat, Oliver would get up and move slowly to the side aisle, make his way out of the sanctuary and out the side door of the foyer.

(OLIVER *gets up, slowly moves to side of church, seems surprised, and stops.)*

NARRATOR: One Sunday, though, when they were resetting the stained-glass windows, Oliver's way was blocked. He was forced to use the middle aisle.

(OLIVER *and parishioners move to the center aisle, simulating conversation with one another. They take their cues from the narrator's story.)*

NARRATOR: Standing in the crowded passageway, several persons said how nice it was to see him again. A smile broke over Oliver's face as he nodded. *(Restrained joy)* He felt good about that all week long. *(All except* OLIVER, MAYOR, WIFE *leave. They wait in foyer.)* One week, he talked with the Mayor and his wife all the way to the door. *(They exit down center aisle.)* Somehow, as he descended the front steps of the church, Oliver didn't feel poor anymore. The good feeling lasted all the way down the block and up the stairs to his one-room apartment above the hardware store.

(PARISHIONERS *including* OLIVER, *reenter, taking various places.* OLIVER *sits in front pew left.)*

NARRATOR: One Sunday, when he was sitting in the very front, the minister asked him if he could stay on for a few minutes.

(MINISTER *and* OLIVER *stand, talking softly, in front of first pew.)*

MINISTER: So it's settled then?

OLIVER: Yes, sir.

MINISTER *(happily):* Good. We've been needing an assistant maintenance man. I should have thought of you sooner.

(MINISTER *exits to foyer.)*

NARRATOR: There was a new spring to Oliver's step after that. His main job was inside the church, making sure everything was neat and polished. On Saturday nights, he would go back and forth through the pews (OLIVER *does so),* making sure all the hymnals were in place and the pencils sharpened. Very often he was tempted. One night, when he was replacing pencils in the second pew, he removed a hymnal from the rack (OLIVER *does so).*

OLIVER: It must be here somewhere! I've searched nearly every place. *(He looks up toward the front, then replaces the unopened hymnal. Walking up into the chancel platform area, he stops and looks off to his left.)*

NARRATOR: Oliver turned his thoughts to the previous year. Back to when the church had decided to replace the worn hymnals with brand new ones.

That is when he had first begun to save. At first, it was only pennies and an occasional nickel. Soon, he filled the small jar in his bedroom with coins. Finally, his savings now in a mayonnaise jar, Oliver had gone to the storekeeper below his small room and exchanged the coins for dollar bills. Later that day, when he saw the church secretary leave for lunch, Oliver slipped into the room where the new hymnals were kept. Carefully, he removed one from the big cardboard box on the floor. Reaching into his pocket, he took the 12 dollar bills and put them inside the cover. Oliver placed the book back in the box and went home. A few weeks later, the church bulletin printed the names of all the people who had donated funds to purchase the new hymnals. Praise was duly given and duly accepted. Oliver read through the whole list, knowing his own name would not be printed there. But with the passing of time, he had grown curious. Week after week, he had moved about the church, hunting for a particular hymnal.

(OLIVER *shrugs his shoulders, comes down from the chancel platform, and takes an aisle seat in the second pew on the left.* PARISHIONERS *[except two] enter and sit in the first and second pews on the right.)*

NARRATOR: So now it all came down to this Sunday. Oliver was glad he had resisted the temptation to go through all the books while he was alone in the church. He sat there by himself. *(Two* PARISHIONERS *come up the center aisle.)* Oliver stared at the hymnal in the rack in front of him. Something told him the long search was over. *(The two* PARISHIONERS *stop at his pew.)*

PARISHIONER: Excuse us, please.

OLIVER *(looking up):* Oh, yes, excuse me. *(He slides over to the middle of the pew, away from the hymnal.)*

PARISHIONER *(reaches out, takes hymnal from rack and opens it):* How nice! *(Shows it to* PARISHIONER *No. 2 who is seated beside her.)* Look on the inside cover.

PARISHIONER No. 2: You mean *here,* on the dedication page?

PARISHIONER: That's it. On the little piece of paper pasted in there.

PARISHIONER No. 2: But where it says "donated by" there isn't any name. All it says is "anonymous donor."

PARISHIONER: That's what I mean—a real Christian. Someone gave this to the church and didn't want any credit for it.

PARISHIONER No. 2: I guess you're right. A real Christian indeed.

NARRATOR: The lady turned toward Oliver and smiled. Sitting there, he wondered if she knew. She couldn't, of course. Nodding, he returned the friendly smile. Oliver's search, the one that had brought him to the congregation's attention, was over. As the organist began to play, Oliver looked up past the altar toward the stained-glass window of Jesus. Bowing his head, he thanked God for the blessings bestowed upon him. Oliver Hurst, the man who did good, was at peace.

*(Everyone stands and leaves the sanctuary as a processional, by the center aisle.)*

*A Caring/Sharing Skit No. 1*
*Presented by and for Senior Adults*

# God the Comforter

## by Orleatha Gravel Kellogg

This presentation may be given by senior adults to nursing home residents, or to a local church group.

**Background Scripture:** John 14:16; 15:26; 2 Corinthians 1:3; Acts 9:31; Romans 15:4; 12:16; 1 Thessalonians 4:16-18; 5:11; 1 Corinthians 13:4; Ephesians 4:4-6

**Props**

two chairs
large patchwork quilt
quilt block sachets to give each person in the audience (if skit is presented in a nursing home)

**Characters**

SCRIPTURE READERS
NARRATOR
EMMA, a nursing home resident
SARAH, another resident

As the play opens, NARRATOR introduces SCRIPTURE READERS, who read the verses listed above.

NARRATOR: There is a common theme to all of these scripture verses we have just heard read. But let's have Emma and Sarah, who live in a nursing home, tell us about God the Comforter.

(SARAH *enters and sits in chair working on a quilt.* EMMA *enters from other side of platform or room. She slowly walks to where* SARAH *sits.* EMMA *mimes knocking at door, then enters before* SARAH *invites her to come in.)*

EMMA: Hello Sarah, want some company? I'm tired of pushing myself up and down that hall.

SARAH: Come in, Emma. I've got something to show you. *(Holds up quilt)* Look at this!

EMMA: So, it's a quilt.

SARAH: Not just a quilt, Emma! My quilt! My mama made it for me when I got married over 60 years ago.

EMMA: It sure is old. What are you going to do with it? You sure don't need it in this place.

SARAH: No, I don't. I have plenty of warm bedding here. My daughter brought this quilt over about an hour ago. She thought I'd enjoy seeing it again. See, she has mended it and restored it so it looks like new. She thought I would like to give it to my granddaughter for a wedding present.

EMMA: Young people want fancy things, Sarah, not old cast-off stuff like that old quilt.

SARAH: Not my granddaughter! She respects things out of the past. She has had her eye on this comforter for a long time now. She calls it a family heirloom.

EMMA: That old quilt? An heirloom? Come on, Sarah, you're a bit tetched today.

SARAH: No I'm not, Emma. Look at this quilt. It's got a story to tell. Remember those cold bedrooms we slept in as children?

EMMA: I sure do! And when I was a bride, Sarah, I still slept in a cold bedroom! Without warm comforters, such as this one, we would have been frozen to death!

SARAH: I remember how the women of the neighborhood would get together to make quilts. Several ladies would come to our house to help Mama so she would have quilts for the winter. Then Mama took her turn to go help the other women. What a good time they had working together! Their mouths were going as fast as their needles!

EMMA: Yes, they sure did enjoy the fellowship. But, Sarah, you and I made a lot of quilts in our day. With three girls I had plenty of sewing to do, and so I always had lots of scraps left over to work up into quilts. I guess all those quilts are spread out among the family now. *(Fingers quilt)* It sure is a pretty quilt. Wonder why they called this the crazy quilt pattern?

SARAH: I don't know. Maybe because it makes no rhyme or reason with all the different patches and shapes and colors. It was one way to use up scraps, as you said, and that wasn't crazy. But look, Emma, what has happened to these once insignificant scraps. Each is different, yet each is important for each adds color and pattern, all blending together to make a beautiful, warm comforter. In a way this quilt is like us Christians. We're all so different, yet we are one in Christ because—

EMMA: Now, Sarah, you're not going to talk religion again, are you?

SARAH: Now, Emma, I know that you think God has forgotten about you in this place. But hear me out, please. This comforter helped keep me and my husband warm on those cold winter nights long ago. It made us comfortable so we could sleep and get some rest. And God is like that, too, Emma. He is our Comforter in the chilly times of our lives. He covers us with the warmth of His love.

EMMA: I sure don't feel God is here at all, Sarah.

SARAH: Emma, let me remind you of something. Jesus told His disciples, just before He was raised up into the heavens, that He would not leave them without comfort, but would send the Holy Spirit to comfort them. Emma, we have inherited that promise!

EMMA: I don't know, Sarah. This place isn't like the world out there.

SARAH: No, it's not, Emma. It wasn't intended to be. It's a special place created to fill the special needs of special people like you and me. Just as this quilt is made up of patches, all different, so we are different here in this nursing home. We all have our different needs. The patches of this quilt were just laying around with no use until someone took them and sewed them together, took more material and made a lining and an inner lining. All these are held together by these ties made from yarn. Together, all these materials are useful and pretty, too. God does the same thing with Christians. He takes all of us, Emma, as different as we are, and binds us together in His love. He gives us comfort through the Holy Spirit, and even then, He is not through with us. He wants us to comfort each other. When we show love to others we are comforting them just as God comforts us. That's why God gave us each other, Emma, even when we live in a nursing home.

EMMA: I don't know, Sarah.

SARAH: Look at it this way, Emma. This home is a community, and we have neighbors just like we had when we were keeping house and were helping each other out. Why should we stop doing that now?

EMMA: I guess you got a point there, Sarah. You sure have been like a neighbor, and a friend, too.

SARAH: Why, Emma, we are just scraps, scraps of humanity, until God takes us and binds us together in a Christian community. In our community here in the nursing home, we can be useful for Him.

EMMA: Well, I suppose so. What did you have in mind, Sarah?

SARAH: The yarn to tie the quilt must be strong to hold all the layers together. And we too must be strong, Emma, strong in our faith to help each other over the chilly times of life. We get our strength from reading the Bible and praying for ourselves and for each other. That's the warmth in our chilly times just like this comforter gave me warmth in that chilly bedroom. Guess you've just been going through one of those chilly times in life, Emma. All you need to do is to ask for God's comfort.

EMMA: Yes, Sarah, I have been through a chilly time. But you have opened my eyes, and more important, my heart. I do see things differently now. Mama and her neighbors came together to do something useful. They took perfectly good scraps of materials and made warm comforters. And you're right, Sarah, I do have neighbors just like I did when I was living in my home in Hills City. And we can come together right here in this nursing home and do useful things.

SARAH: Oh, Emma, I am so proud of you!

EMMA: I do have a lot of blessings, here, Sarah. A warm bed, loving hands to help me when I can't get in and out of that bed, and there are many caring hands that prepare food for me and clean my room, and many other things. But best of all, I have a good neighbor like you, Sarah.

SARAH: My pleasure, Emma. God is still doing His job as our Comforter no matter where we are. But Emma, we must continue to do our part—to be comforters to others no matter how old we are and no matter where we are.

EMMA: I did think there wasn't anything I could do for the Lord in this place. But there is! I can smile at others and at those who care for me. I can read the Bible, or if someone else isn't too well, then I could read the Bible to her. I can pray for the world and God's people in it. And I can always pray for my neighbors right here in this nursing home, and for all the people, like you and me, Sarah, in other nursing homes in the world. And I mustn't forget to pray for the staff of this nursing home and those who come to visit me. Why, Sarah, I'm going to be awfully busy being a comforter!

SARAH: That's wonderful, Emma. Well, what do you think about my quilt now?

EMMA: I think it's a family heirloom just as your granddaughter claims. And it shouldn't be folded away in a drawer. A comforter's job is to be on a bed giving comfort to people on chilly nights.

SARAH: Just like Christians are supposed to be giving comfort to others, and not just sitting around, heh Emma?

EMMA: Yes indeed, Sarah.

SARAH: Then I will give the quilt to my granddaughter for a wedding present. It will make a lovely gift for her.

EMMA: And thank you, Sarah, for my gift. I'm sorry I was such a doubter. God didn't forget about me, I forgot about him. I hope He will forgive me.

SARAH: He will, Emma. Just ask Him. That's part of His comfort, too.

EMMA: You're right, Sarah. Another thing: God repairs us just like your daughter repaired that old quilt. By being forgiven we can go on forgiving others who hurt us. That's another way to be a comforter. Oh, Sarah, I'm so excited about our talk. There are so many ways to be comforters, and—oh, that reminds me, I've got to go now. Excuse me, but I must go down the hall and talk to Helen, my new neighbor. She just moved in a few days ago and I know that she needs some comfort.

SARAH: If you don't mind, I'll go along with you. I haven't met the new member of our community, either.

**Suggested Song:** "Blest Be the Tie That Binds"

## Quilt Block Sachet Instructions

*(As a surprise, you may wish to give each nursing home guest a quilt block sachet.)*

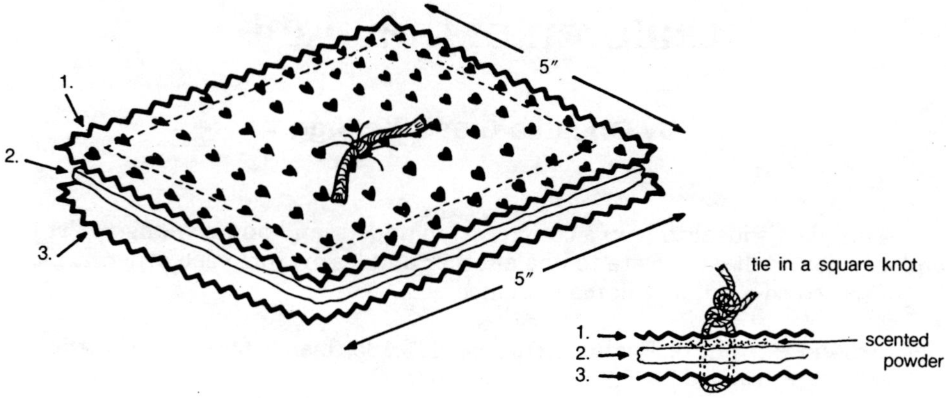


Use any colorful scraps of fabric. A piece 5 ″ x 5″ makes up into a nice workable size block. Use pinking shears to cut, then put squares together with a piece of batting, slightly smaller, in the center. Pour a small amount of sachet powder on the batting before assembling. Leave a ⅝″ margin all around, then tie in the center with a colorful contrasting piece of yarn. Type on a piece of paper 2 Corinthians 1:3*b*-4, and attach to back of block by tacking corners with thread.

---

## Charitable Contributions

We hear criticism that Christianity's big business:
"Give, give, give" is the name of the game.
In my opinion that's the best definition
Of Christian life we could claim!

—*Ruth M. Walsh*

# Children of the Light

## by Orleatha Gravel Kellogg

This play is ideal to help a congregation understand how a younger person and a senior adult can relate to one another and learn from each other. It may be presented to a nursing home audience.

**Background Scripture:** Psalm 27:1; 36:9; 119:105; Isaiah 60:1; Matthew 5:14; John 8:13; Ephesians 5:8

**Props**

unassembled kerosene lamp
small container for kerosene
matches
flame cut from yellow paper (Many nursing homes will not permit actual lighting of the lamp.)
small table
two chairs

**Cast**

SCRIPTURE READER (Optional)
GRANDMOTHER
YOUNG WOMAN

As the play opens, GRANDMOTHER sits on one of the chairs near the small table. YOUNG WOMAN enters.

YOUNG WOMAN: It's me, Grandma. There's been a bad storm and the electricity is off. I came by to see if you are all right.

GRANDMOTHER: Bless you, dear. I'm fine. But it's getting dark and I was beginning to worry about how I was going to get around.

YOUNG WOMAN: You can stop worrying, Grandma. I can stay a while. Surely the lights will go on any minute now. I guess our modern world isn't as self-sufficient as we think. What we need is one of those old kerosene lamps like you had when you were growing up, Grandma. *(Giggles.)*

GRANDMOTHER: Don't laugh. I just might be able to accommodate you. I brought that box down from the attic yesterday, thinking I should try to get rid of some of my clutter. But, somehow, I just couldn't bear to part with that old lamp.

YOUNG WOMAN *(looks in box):* But Grandma, this is just a box of junk!

GRANDMOTHER: Maybe so, dear. My eyes aren't very good anymore, but let's have another look. If I remember correctly we just might be able to put together a lamp out of that junk.

YOUNG WOMAN: It looks hopeless, but if you insist. *(Rummages around in the box, and then holds up glass chimney)* Well, here's the chimney, and it appears to be in good shape.

GRANDMOTHER: Thank goodness for that! The chimney is an important part of the lamp. Its job is to protect the flame from drafts so it won't flutter. Without its protection the lamp won't be able to shine brightly.

YOUNG WOMAN: And here's the wick, at least I think it is. It's a ribbon or woven strip of some kind.

GRANDMOTHER *(taking the strip in her hand, she feels of it):* That's the wick all right. That's very important too. The wick reaches down into the kerosene to feed the flame. Look and see if you can find the adjuster. It's a round metal contraption with a stem to turn the wick up or down.

YOUNG WOMAN: Here it is, Grandma. *(Holds up adjuster. She hands it to the older woman who fumbles with it and the wick. With the help of the younger woman the wick is threaded through the adjuster.)*

YOUNG WOMAN: And here is the base of the lamp, Grandma. Why, here's kerosene and matches. Grandma, you must have forseen the storm and were getting your lamp ready.

GRANDMOTHER: No, it was just as I said. I brought it down from the attic just today. I kept it mostly because I wanted to see if it still works.

YOUNG WOMAN: Well, let's find out. *(Pretends to fill lamp, light it, and then puts chimney in place)* There it is, Grandma! Just like in your parlor when you were a girl!

GRANDMOTHER: I'll have you know that I used this lamp when I kept house with your grandfather. We didn't get electricity until we moved to town in the 50s. Isn't it nice? *(She reaches to adjust the wick.)* Now even with my weak old eyes I'll be able to see where to walk. I won't be afraid to move around in this room. *(Pause)* Oh, the memories that old lamp brings back. Every morning that chimney had to be cleaned. Sometimes someone would turn the wick up too high and the chimney would get smoked. Then it was harder to clean. Hot sudsy water took care of it in no time, and a piece of newspaper was important for a bright light. I had to fill the lamp every day, too. A wick, on the other hand, lasted for months. But it had to be trimmed every so often. We sat around the table using that lamp for light as we read or sewed. That's all the light we had in all our rooms back then. Here I am an old woman, hard of hearing, can hardly see or walk, but there sits that old lamp putting out its light.

YOUNG WOMAN: It's like the light of God, Grandma. His light goes on and on. His light is guidance for us. This room was dark before, and you were afraid to walk about for fear of stumbling. The light has brought you safety and assurance just as God's light does in our lives.

GRANDMOTHER: You're right, dear. And God's light has been in the world from the time of creation. When you're old, as I am, it isn't always easy to remember that God is near. When life walks in the dark, it's hard to believe that He has not forgotten. But He said, "Let there be light," and in hard times I remember that God reveals himself in darkness, today as well as He did then.

YOUNG WOMAN: The Lord is our Light, Grandma.

GRANDMOTHER: Yes, and the Bible also tells us that He is a Lamp for our feet and a Light for our path. I'm not able to go out into the world much anymore but I can still pray for God's world and for the people in it.

YOUNG WOMAN: Grandma, that's letting your light shine for Jesus. Remember, Jesus told his followers, "You are the light of the world." Whenever we sing or speak of God's love to others we are letting our light shine. Or when we smile at others or pray for them we are letting our light shine.

GRANDMOTHER: Yes, the Scripture has much to say about God's light. Jesus also told us to walk as children of light and He would give us light. He does this through His Holy Spirit, who is like a shield around us helping our lights shine brightly in the same way the chimney protects the flame of a lamp.

YOUNG WOMAN: And Grandma, God cleans our chimneys with His forgiveness when we get them all smoked up with sin.

GRANDMOTHER: He certainly does! Just as this lamp must be filled with fuel every day, so must we trust God to fill us every day with His love and strength by reading our Bibles and praying. That's the only way our lights will be bright with His love.

YOUNG WOMAN: And Grandma, when we allow Jesus to have charge of our lives, it's like adjusting the wick up so the light shines brighter. But when we try to have our own way, or try to get along without Jesus, then the wick is turned down, and we are only a dim light.

GRANDMOTHER: Remember, dear, the wick can't shine by itself. It must draw up fuel, but it has to be the proper fuel. And to have fuel for our lights, we have to dip our wicks in the Holy Spirit, in the Scriptures, and in prayer. *(Leans back and sighs)* This old lamp, in many ways, is a lot like God wants us to be. It was just a box of junk. Maybe that's all we would be if we didn't allow God to put us together properly as lamps. Then He can use us as light for others to see His love. *(Pause)* This old lamp used to give out light many years ago, but right now we just gave it another chance to shine again. God does that for us, too. He doesn't want us to be lamps that shine only once in a while. He wants us to shine for Him every day.

YOUNG WOMAN: The electricity is on! *(She looks at the lamp, and touches the stem of the adjuster.)* Oh, Grandma, don't ever give this lamp away. It will always remind me of our talk about what it means to be light—to shine for Jesus knowing that He will supply the fuel for our flames.

**Suggested Songs:** "Lead Kindly Light," "The Light of the World Is Jesus."

If this play is presented to a nursing home audience, you may wish to leave a gift bookmark for each person present.

**Instructions for Bookmark**

Purchase venetian blind repair webbing or rug tape. Either resembles the texture of a lamp wick. Use a black or colored magic marker (fine line) for lettering. Example below:

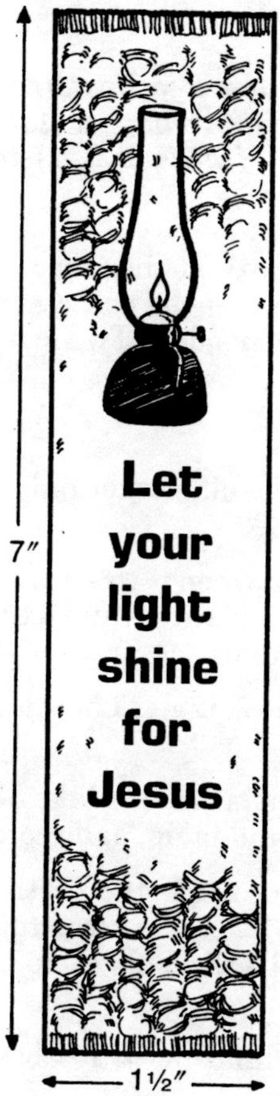


## Just a Reminder

Tired minds in trying hour,
Lean on Him, for He has power
To expel the anguish we possess
With a loving, guiding tenderness.
Have faith and overcome the plight,
And use the strength—the gracious might
That man's been offered since time began,
To his creation—the earthly plan.

*—Gary Ward*

## Make a Memory

Make a memory, do something special,
Leave the dust upon the shelf.
Ignore that broom, stash the dishes,
Take some time just for yourself.

All too quickly time is passing,
Turn on your creativity;
Find a new and different adventure
Then seize your opportunity.

Avoid the timid or halfhearted,
Plunge right in with all your zest;
Life is to be lived and enjoyed,
With enthusiasm do your best.

Each day is a gift from God;
Be wise as you fulfill your duty;
Plan ahead for the essentials,
But schedule in some beauty.

Why sit around, moan, and complain?
Go ahead, design an exciting scheme;
Make a memory for your treasure,
You can activate your dream!

*—Elaine Hardt*

# His Leaf Shall Not Wither

**by Donna Fletcher Crow**

*(On stage are two "human" leaves. They may be readers wearing large autumn leaves cut from brown paper, or dressed as puppets behind a puppet stage. Leaf 1 is a female, leaf 2 is a male. Narrator stands to side of stage or is offstage with microphone.)*

NARRATOR: The leaves were falling from the great oak at the meadow's edge. They were falling from all the trees. One branch of the oak reached high above the others and stretched far out over the meadow. Two leaves clung to its very tip.

LEAF 1: It isn't the way it used to be.

LEAF 2: No, so many of us have fallen off tonight we're almost the only ones left on our branch.

LEAF 1: You never know who's going to go next. Even when it was warm and the sun shone, a storm or a cloudburst would come sometimes and many leaves were torn off, though they were still young. You just never know.

LEAF 2: The sun seldom shines now, and when it does it gives no warmth. We must have warmth again.

LEAF 1: Can it be true, can it really be true, that others come to take our places when we're gone, and after them, still others, and more, and more?

NARRATOR: Generations come and generations go, while the earth endures forever. The sun rises and the sun goes down, back it returns to its place and rises there again. The wind blows south, the wind blows north, round and round it goes and returns full circle.

LEAF 2: It is really true. We can't even begin to imagine it; it's beyond our powers.

LEAF 1: It makes me very sad. *(Pause)* Why must we fall?

LEAF 2: What happens to us when we have fallen?

LEAF 1: We sink down . . .

LEAF 2: What is under us?

NARRATOR: I am He who has carried you from the womb until you grow old. And when white hairs come, I will carry you still. I have made you and I will carry you and bring you to safety.

LEAF 1: Do you suppose white hairs are the same as brown edges?

LEAF 2: Don't worry so much about it. You're trembling.

LEAF 1: That's nothing. I tremble at the least thing now. I don't feel so sure of my hold as I used to.

NARRATOR: I have been young and am now grown old, and never have I seen a righteous man forsaken. Day in, day out, he lends generously and his children become a blessing.

LEAF 1: Let's remember how beautiful it was, how wonderful, when the sun came out and shone so warmly that we thought we'd burst with life. Do you remember? And the morning dew, and the mild and splendid nights . . .

LEAF 2: Now the nights are dreadful, and there is no end to them.

NARRATOR: My thoughts went back to times long past. I remember forgotten years. All night long I was in deep distress, as I lay thinking, my spirit was sunk in despair. But then, O Lord, I call to mind thy deeds; I recall thy wonderful acts in times gone by. I meditate upon thy works and muse on all thou has done. O God, thy way is holy.

LEAF 1: Have I changed much?

LEAF 2: Not in the least. You only think so because I've gotten to be so yellow and ugly. But it's different in your case.

LEAF 1: You're fooling me.

LEAF 2: No, really. Believe me, you're as lovely as the day you were born. Here and there may be a little yellow spot but it's hardly noticeable and only makes you handsomer, believe me.

LEAF 1: Thanks. I don't believe you. Not altogether. But thank you for saying so anyway.

NARRATOR: Blessed is the man who trusts in the Lord and rests his confidence upon Him. He is like a tree planted beside a watercourse which yields its fruit in season and its leaf never withers.

---

## Proper Paragon

The pillar of the congregation
  Shook hands with the pastor, aglow.
"Wonderful sermon!" she gushed and affused,
  "Everything applies to someone I know!"

*—Ruth M. Walsh*

# Gather the Wheat into His Barn

by Donna Fletcher Crow

*(A child sits on* Grandpa's *lap, looking at photo album. Or, consider using a large doll as a ventriloquist's dummy for dialogue.)*

CHILD: Tell me about this one, Grandpa.

GRANDPA: That was the wheat harvest of 1927. I worked in it with my dad that year.

CHILD: Why did it take all those horses just to pull one machine?

GRANDPA: We started out with 33 head of horses and mules, but had to add 7 more that year because the ground was too soft from lack of winter rain to pack it down. The next year that old horse-drawn header was replaced with two machines pulled by tractors—they could harvest a field in three or four weeks, about half the time it took the horses and mules.

CHILD: But then the horses and mules didn't have a job, did they?

GRANDPA: That's right, *[child's name]*, but harvesting faster helped avoid the danger of a windstorm blowing up to shell out the wheat, or a fire in the field, or rain stopping the work.

CHILD: Tell me what it was like, Grandpa.

GRANDPA: Well, we were up at 5:30 to feed and harness the mules and horses, then came in for breakfast. We were in the field by 7 and worked until 6:30 in the evening. We took an hour and a half off for lunch because the horses needed rest and they had to be taken into the barn for food and water. It was dusty, itchy, and always very, very hot—about 105 degrees.

CHILD: But tell me more about the horses and mules, Grandpa.

GRANDPA: Mules were smarter than horses and better to work with. Mules had more "horse sense" and wouldn't work themselves to death. When a horse gets overtired it gets keyed up and works until it drops. Mules would just slow down. The driver said if a horse fell uphill he was just goofing off, but if he fell downhill, he was all in and couldn't go any farther. Mules wouldn't injure themselves by fighting and kicking like horses. Horses were also more likely to get sore shoulders from horse collars and require doctoring, mules were tougher. Mules also wouldn't overheat and overdrink as horses will.

CHILD *(points to picture):* Why isn't anyone riding this horse?

GRANDPA: We always led one saddled horse behind the header machine in case it broke down. Then someone could ride for repairs. Or if one of the horses or mules got sick or fell down, we took the saddle off, put him in harness, and went right on working.

CHILD: What did you and you daddy do?

GRANDPA: My dad—that's your great-grandpa—was the machine man. He was the highest paid on the crew. He earned $15.00 a day. It was his job to keep the machine working. I got $5.00 a day for running the grain elevator. That was big money; before harvesttime we got $1.00 a day for working in summer fallow.

CHILD: I sure like it when you tell me stories, Grandpa.

GRANDPA: That's good, *[child's name],* because I like telling 'em. Shall I tell you another story about a wheat harvest?

CHILD: Sure. Does it have horses in it, too?

GRANDPA: No, this is one Jesus told, and they harvested wheat by hand in those days.

CHILD: Wheat sure is *old,* isn't it, Grandpa?

GRANDPA: I guess it's about one of the oldest foods on earth, *[name].* Anyway, Jesus said that the kingdom of heaven is like a man who planted good seed in his field and while everyone was asleep, an enemy came and sowed weeds. When the weeds showed up, the man's servants said, "You sowed good wheat in the field. Where did all those weeds come from? Shall we pull them out?" And the farmer said, "An enemy planted those weeds, but don't pull them up yet because if you do you might pull up some of the wheat, too. Let them grow together until harvestime, then I will tell the harvesters to pull up the weeds first and tie them in bundles to throw in the fire, then gather the wheat and put it in my barn."

Do you know what Jesus meant by the story, *[name]?*

CHILD *(shaking head):* huh-uh.

GRANDPA: Jesus is telling us that good people and evil people live together in the world, but someday He will come back and pull out the evil people and take the people who love Him to heaven with Him. Who do you think the enemy in the story is?

CHILD: The devil?

GRANDPA: That's right, and that story is to remind you not to listen to him so you won't get pulled out with the weeds.

CHILD: Thank you, Grandpa. I don't think I'll ever forget that.

# A Monologue

**by Eva Campbell**

It was barely dawn when I awoke with a feeling of eagerness. I dressed hurriedly and woke my sister, Doris.

"Tell your grandmother I'll be over this afternoon to help with the peaches," Mother said as she handed us a piece of bread and butter. Then she returned to the yeast bread she was making. It was 1936, a depression year. Food was scarce and new clothes unheard of, but I doubt that there were two happier children anywhere.

We crossed the yard. I glanced back at the sound of Brownie barking. The three-room house stood staunchly, as if to brace itself against the promise of a hot August day. Back of the house a lone, flaunting apple tree stood guard over a lackluster chicken house. Scattered leghorns pecked at the earth.

We proceeded down the thirsty path that led through the bloated peach orchard, its fruits now mature, lending a sweet-smelling aroma. The bulging branches hung heavily. A gnawing began in my stomach. I reached for one of the orchard's prized produce. In my eagerness to make contact, I broke through the fuzziness and it yielded its juice contents down my thumb and wrists. I jerked out the stem, securely placed both thumbs in its void and split the peach in two. The seed dropped, abandoned, as Doris and I shared its sweet deliciousness.

The orchard, which was a hyphen between our small farm and the hill farm of our grandparents, ended. My nostrils caught the redolence of honeysuckle, mingled with the rank odor of the pigpen. A slight old man beckoned feebly from a nearby field of almost ripe grain. We hurried in his direction and the loving touch that had momentarily belonged to the field was transferred to us. His knees made a crackling sound as he bent to encircle me in his arms. He chuckled as his dry hand took my moist one and he led me toward the house.

The next couple of hours were spent with a mixture of chatter, laughs, biscuits, and jelly.

The sun was boiling when we started home. We reached the fence that led to the orchard. I was just over the fence when Doris grabbed my arm and screamed. The ground before us was covered, literally covered, with giant-sized worms. There was hardly a place to step without squashing one. Since I had holes in the soles of my shoes and Doris didn't, we decided she would carry me on her back. Every step was slow and not too sure as we made our way home. About every 10 paces came a reassuring "I won't" to the demand, "Don't drop me! Don't drop me!"

I don't recall if we had other encounters with the worms. I do remember Mother's remark that day. "These are called armyworms. This means the ground will be used for military purposes some day."

In 1941 construction began for Camp Atterbury, which is still being used for military purposes. The hill in Bartholomew County is desolate now. The only time we get near it is when we visit the cemetery where members of our family are buried.

When we do, I like to sit and reminisce. I recall how much I loved my Sunday School teacher. I remember Daddy carrying me through the woods to church services. I think about another prophecy made hundreds of years before it came to pass, concerning the birth of Jesus. But it did come to pass and now we have the promise of everlasting life.

I sit and wonder silently
What does the future hold for me?
Eternal joy to have or lose—
It's waiting there; I only choose.

"For God so loved the world, that he gave his only begotten Son, that whosoever believeth in him should not perish, but have everlasting life" (John 3:16).

Let not His death be in vain. Let us have that life!

---

## Limits

Christ will give himself to us;
Fill us to the brim . . .
Limited only by the measure
That we give ourselves to Him.

*—Ruth M. Walsh*

## Conviction

To know Christ is to become aware
Of the contradiction, to a finite degree,
Between what I am in sin,
And what, in Him, I may be.

*—Ruth M. Walsh*

# A Merry Heart

**by Dorothy M. Brubaker**

**Characters:**

MR. LEADER *(chairs the meeting)*
MR. AGREE
MRS. AGREE
MRS. MIRTH
MRS. PIOUS *(a severe looking woman)*

*(Characters are seated around the table so that each faces the audience.)*

MR. LEADER: Mrs. Pious wishes to speak to our program committee before we begin plans for our next fellowship. Mrs. Pious.

MRS. PIOUS: I felt it my duty to report that last month's program was unsuitable for people our age. Imagine what visitors were thinking—old folk dressed like Mother Goose characters! It was so indignified!

MR. LEADER: The subject of suitability is open for discussion.

MR. AGREE: Speaking of the reaction of visitors, we brought neighbors. They enjoyed the fellowship so much that they are coming to Sunday School and church services. They say they like the friendly atmosphere of our fellowships.

MR. LEADER: My sister and her husband from Iowa were visiting us. They came to the fellowship with us. They plan to use the idea in their fellowship.

MRS. AGREE: I was feeling rather blue that day. The fellowship lifted my spirits. I don't deny that we are old, but folk our age need a little fun once in a while. Being old in years doesn't mean we can't be young at heart.

MRS. PIOUS: We are old and pretending to be young is just foolish.

MRS. MIRTH: Throughout the Bible we find that God wants us to be merry, to have a cheerful countenance. I found this scripture and tacked it up on my frig: "Go thy way, eat thy bread with joy, and . . . with a merry heart; for God now accepteth thy works, Ecclesiastes 9:7."

MR. LEADER: I have found nothing unchristian in our programs. Our function is to make available an opportunity for fellowship in a Christian environment. This applies not only to our members, but all senior adults in our community. Mr. Agree has pointed out that it was a means of bringing unchurched neighbors into the church.

MRS. PIOUS: We should be spending our time in Bible study groups, prayer meetings, church services.

MR. LEADER: We do all of those things, but our monthly fellowships are for relaxation and good clean fun. At the fellowships, people feel free to drop facades—to be themselves.

MR. AGREE: Somewhere I read that "a dour religion is Satan's tool."

MRS. AGREE: I watched a Christian TV program the other day. The pastor said that a woman who was deeply depressed came to him for counseling, and he advised her to go home, look at herself in the mirror, and laugh out loud 10 times. She was to do this for several days.

MRS. PIOUS: Ridiculous!

MRS. AGREE *(continues):* The pastor said he saw the woman a few weeks later. She was smiling and looked so much younger. He asked her how she was feeling. She said she felt fine, that her depression was gone. Then she asked, "Where did you learn of that cure?" The pastor replied, "From the Bible. Proverbs 17:22 says, 'A merry heart doeth good like a medicine.'"

MR. LEADER: It appears that we believe our fellowships are quite scriptural and a valid ministry. Are we in agreement.

MRS. PIOUS: I certainly do not agree with your opinion. I have done my duty. *(She exits.)*

---

## Stewardquip

As Christians we take no anxious thought
For the morrow or what might be brewing:
The idea is to be good stewards—
But minus all the "stewing."

*—Ruth M. Walsh*

# Let the Children Come

**by Dorothy M. Brubaker**

**Characters:**

MR. ARNOLD
MRS. JAMES
MR. OWENS
MR. CHARLES
MISS BROWN
MRS. MORROW
MR. DAVID

*(Seven elderly persons are seated at a table facing audience.)*

MR. ARNOLD: I've called this special meeting of the Senior Adult Committee to consider complaints concerning the present system for children's worship. We should discuss the matter before presenting complaints to the church council. Miss Brown, Mrs. Morrow, Mr. David, and Mr. Charles, may we hear your complaints?

MISS BROWN: I find it very difficult to enjoy the service when it is disrupted by the children. Is it necessary to have them come into the church service? Why can't they be kept downstairs?

MRS. JAMES: We believe that the children should become familiar with worship in the sanctuary if only for the short period of the children's sermon.

MISS BROWN: Even so, they manage to cause so much disturbance. Sometimes I'm so upset I can't enjoy the sermon.

MR. CHARLES: I don't mind having the kids in the service. My objection is that having a children's sermon takes extra time and makes us late getting out of the service. That makes me late for my Sunday afternoon golf game. The guys at the club don't like to be kept waiting. Why can't the kids listen to the pastor's sermon same as we do?

MRS. MORROW: I agree that the service is too long. My husband complains about a late dinner. He likes Sunday dinner promptly at 12.

MR. DAVID: Perhaps they could just have the entire children's service downstairs. They wouldn't need to come to the sanctuary at all. I've missed some good ball games because we got home late.

MRS. JAMES: I have something special to show you. *(Lights lowered, a slide of Jesus with little children is flashed on the screen.)*

VOICE *(live or prerecorded):* Jesus said, "Suffer little children, and forbid them not, to come unto me: for of such is the kingdom of heaven. And he laid his hands on them . . ." (Matthew 19:14-15*a*).

*(A second slide shows a group of little ones singing, "Jesus Loves the Little Children." Lights come on.)*

MRS. JAMES *(continues):* All of you, with the exception of Miss Brown, have grandchildren. Have you considered their need to learn to worship with adults in the sanctuary?

MR. OWENS: I agree with Mrs. James. I enjoy seeing the youngsters in church. They need to feel that they are a part of the family of God. Retired folk have all week for golf and TV. I figure one day spent worshiping God can't be considered a sacrifice.

MR. CHARLES: You're right, Jim. Guess I never realized how selfish we can become. You'll hear no more complaints from me.

MRS. MORROW: This really has been a revelation to me. Jake will just have to wait for Sunday dinner until I get home, or else he can take me out to dinner.

MR. ARNOLD: Thank you, Mrs. James, for a very meaningful and helpful presentation. Are we all agreed that we have no recommendation for change of the present system for children's church?

EVERYONE *(except* MISS BROWN*):* Aye!

---

## Eyewitnesses

As we age, we're all aware
Our eyesight may possibly fail;
But we also know, as Christians,
That our vision will prevail!

*—Ruth M. Walsh*

## Shar-ity?

Real charity doesn't
Give a jot
Whether it's tax deductible
Or not!

*—Ruth M. Walsh*

# Love Thy Neighbor

**by Dorothy M. Brubaker**

**Characters:**

MATTIE
ALICE

*(*MATTIE *is resting on a chaise lounge on her patio.)*

ALICE *(enters and sits down):* Mattie, have you seen the new family that moved in down the street? John says they are Cambodian refugees. Imagine what that means to this neighborhood. I hear the church on the corner is allowing the family to live in that house rent free.

MATTIE: I met the Langs. I took some fresh-baked bread over this morning and welcomed them to the neighborhood.

ALICE: Mattie! I can't believe you welcomed them to our neighborhood. They don't even speak our language.

MATTIE: Our Lord commanded that we love our neighbor. If I live according to His will, I must share Christian love with everyone. Psalm 15:1, 3 says, "Lord, who shall abide in thy tabernacle? And who shall dwell in thy holy hill? He that backbiteth not with his tongue, nor doeth evil to his neighbour, nor taketh up a reproach against his neighbour."

ALICE: Now, Mattie, I just don't believe that neighbor means we should associate with them.

MATTIE: Them?

ALICE: You know, the heathen.

MATTIE: Alice, you haven't even met the Langs. Mr. Lang taught in one of the colleges in Cambodia. Mrs. Lang is an accomplished pianist. They speak excellent English, and they are Christians.

ALICE: Maybe this family is different. But what about all those boat people? They bring in disease, they take jobs our people need, and they use welfare funds intended for needy Americans.

MATTIE: The Bible says those who have much will be required by God to give account for much. Have you ever stopped to consider what terrible hardships those refugees suffer? In order to escape persecution and death they left their homes with nothing but the clothes on their backs. They escaped to another country only to be refused haven. Many of them are Christians. They must wonder if Christianity is worth dying for when so-called Christians refuse to help them. Would we be as brave as they if we were in similar circumstances. I wonder.

ALICE: I'm glad I live in a free country where things like that don't happen.

MATTIE: Just suppose we were invaded by Communists.

ALICE: That could never happen here.

MATTIE: Just suppose it did. What would you do?

ALICE: I don't want to think of such a thing. It sends shivers all over me.

MATTIE: Then think about this. There is a portion of scripture that makes God's will very clear. *(She picks up Bible from table and opens it.)* Yes, here it is. Matthew 25:34-40. Listen to this: "Then shall the King say unto them on his right hand, Come, ye blessed of my Father, inherit the kingdom prepared for you from the foundation of the world: for I was an hungred, and ye gave me meat: I was thirsty, and ye gave me drink: I was a stranger, and ye took me in: Naked, and ye clothed me: I was sick, and ye visited me: I was in prison, and ye came unto me. Then shall the righteous answer him, saying, Lord, when saw we thee an hungred, and fed thee? or thirsty, and gave thee drink? When saw we thee a stranger, and took thee in? or naked, and clothed thee? . . . And the King shall answer . . . Inasmuch as ye have done it unto one of the least of these . . . ye have done it unto me."

---

## Balance of Nature

In these days of accent on ecology,
With the earth sciences often chosen,
Perhaps sin should be
Labeled soul erosion!

*—Ruth M. Walsh*

# Into the Fold

**by Dorothy M. Brubaker**

**Characters:**

**Scene 1**

NARRATOR
MRS. BEA LONELY
MRS. CLIMBER
MRS. AMBITION
MRS. GOSSIP
MRS. FIXIT
TWO OTHER PERSONS

**Scene 2**

MRS. BEA LONELY
MRS. ELSIE FRIENDLY
MR. BOB FRIENDLY
MRS. MARGE GRACIOUS
TWO OR THREE PERSONS IN BACKGROUND

## Scene 1

*(The setting is a clubhouse. Characters are seated in two rows.* MRS. BEA LONELY and MRS. ALICE AMBITION *are on the front row with the narrator.* MRS. GOSSIP and MRS. FIXIT *on back row with two other persons.)*

NARRATOR: Mrs. Bea Lonely, a widow, moves to a mobile home community hoping to find new friends. The manager suggests that she visit a meeting of the social club. We look in on that meeting.

MRS. CLIMBER: Ladies, we have two new residents to introduce today. Mrs. Alice Ambition comes to us from Palm Springs. Her husband is a retired Air Force major. Alice has traveled extensively in the United States and abroad. She is past president of the Palm Springs Aspirations Club, a member of the country club, and an officer of the Successful Writers Club. What a wonderful addition to our community! *(Women clap and gather around* MRS. AMBITION.)

MRS. CLIMBER: Ladies! *(They quiet down and go back to their seats.)* Then we also have Mrs. Bea Lonely, a *widow.*

MRS. GOSSIP *(in stage whisper):* Not another widow!

MRS. FIXIT *(in stage whisper):* We certainly don't need more widows here! *(Everyone gathers in clusters of two and three.* MRS. LONELY *is ignored. They all leave and she stands alone. She wanders over to the bulletin board and reads for a few moments silently; then with excitement reads aloud.)*

BEA LONELY: "Invitation to men and women 55+. Come to our friendly fellowship, Main Street Church." *(Her voice fades as curtain closes.)*

## Scene 2

*(Man and woman stand at door greeting people as they arrive. Two or three persons circulate in background.)*

MRS. FRIENDLY *(as* MRS. LONELY *enters):* Welcome to our fellowship. I'm Elsie Friendly. *(She smiles and shakes* MRS. LONELY'S *hand.)*

MRS. LONELY: I'm Bea Lonely. I've just moved to this area.

MR. FRIENDLY: I'm Bob Friendly. *(He smiles and shakes hands.)*

MRS. FRIENDLY: We're so glad you could come. *(She calls to woman standing nearby.)* Marge! *(The woman comes to the door.)* Marge Gracious, meet Bea Lonely. Bea is a newcomer to our area.

MARGE: Welcome, Bea. Is your husband with you?

MRS. LONELY: I'm a widow.

MARGE: So am I. We have several widows in this group.

MRS. LONELY: Do the married couples in the group make the widows welcome?

MARGE: Oh, yes. This is a very special group of Christians. You will like them. All the activities are planned in such a manner as to discourage pairing off or forming cliques. We are all members of the family of God. You will surely find a sincere welcome here. Our Sunday School classes, Bible study groups, and Sunday worship services will also make you feel welcome. We hope you will make this your church home.

MRS. LONELY: I have been looking in all the wrong places for acceptance. This is where I have found it. *(They walk off arm in arm.)*

**Group, Solo, or Duet:** "The Family of God," or similar song.

# Bridle the Tongue

### by Dorothy M. Brubaker

**Characters:**

RUTH
ANNIE
ROSIE
ALICE
BEA

*(Women are seated around a table making craft items.)*

RUTH: Ladies. I have a new item we can make for our missionary society Christmas boutique. It's a toy for babies. It's soft, has no parts that could harm the baby. *(She holds toy for all to see, then passes it to woman nearest her; each passes it on to the next woman.)*

ROSIE: Isn't it cute?

ALICE: Ruth, I believe there is some pastel flannel in the supply cupboard. It would be just right for making these toys.

RUTH: I'll go upstairs and check the cupboard. If we have the flannel, we can start on these today. *(She exits.)*

ANNIE *(rushes in out of breath):* Sorry I'm late. But wait 'til you hear the news! Gen Baker said she couldn't come today because the Williamses invited her to go on a picnic with them. She was baking a cake.

ROSIE: That's news?

ANNIE: Haven't you heard? Sally Williams' brother, Bill, is visiting them, and Gen is running after him.

ROSIE: So that's why Gen is putting a rinse on her hair.

ALICE: I noticed she had on a new outfit at the fellowship. I thought it was far too youthful for her mature figure.

BEA: Annie, I thought you went to the musical with Bill Williams.

ANNIE: I did. Gen knows that. I think she is jealous of me.

ALICE: Sally told me that Gen goes to the spa with her. They are trying to lose weight.

ROSIE: Aren't we all?

ANNIE: Well, I can think of better things to do with my time.

BEA: If I could afford it, I'd go. I think Gen looks great since she started the classes.

ANNIE: I haven't noticed any change. She looks dumpy to me. I think Bill is just trying to be nice to her because she and Sally are friends. It seems to me . . .

RUTH *(entering room):* Ladies! Please remember we are supposed to be Christians.

ROSIE: Ruth, why do you always take up for Gen?

RUTH: Rosie. I remember when Gen brought in meals for your family when you were in the hospital last winter.

RUTH *(slowly):* Well—yes, she did.

RUTH: And Alice, didn't Gen clean your house this spring when you sprained your wrist?

ALICE: Yes, she did. I'd forgotten about that.

RUTH: Annie, perhaps you should admit that you are jealous of Gen. You know she isn't running after Bill. Gossip can cause so much trouble and heartache. Don't you remember what happened to Mary because of vicious gossip? It destroyed her marriage and not a word of it was true.

ALICE: I think we are all too quick to gossip. Gen has done nothing wrong. I'm sorry I talked about her.

ANNIE: You're right, Ruth. I really am jealous of Gen. I'm sorry.

ROSIE: I think we should all make a vow to pay a fine of 10 cents each time we start to gossip.

BEA: Well I didn't gossip this time.

ALICE: I did. Here's my dime.

OTHERS: Here's mine. *(They put coins on table.)*

RUTH: Paying a fine isn't enough. It's more important to ask God to forgive us when we gossip. The Bible has much to say about gossip. Psalm 39:1 says, "I said, I will take heed to my ways, that I sin not with my tongue; I will keep my mouth with a bridle." And Proverbs 12:18 says, "There is one whose rash words are like sword and thrusts, but the tongue of the wise brings healing."

ALICE: We do need prayer for forgiveness. Ruth, would you lead us in prayer?

RUTH *(stands, all bow heads):* Dear Heavenly Father, we ask Your forgiveness . . .

# And Had Compassion

**by Dorothy M. Brubaker**

**Characters:**

MR. DELANEY, a nicely dressed, well groomed, elderly blind man. He holds a white cane.

SAM GOOD

## Scene 1

MR. DELANEY *(sits on bench along a busy street)*

MR. DELANEY *(hearing footsteps):* Please help me! I'm blind. I need help.

SAM GOOD *(approaches cautiously):* Did you say you are blind?

MR. DELANEY: Yes, I'm blind. I'm lost and need help. Please help me. If you can't, would you please call the police to help me? I've been sitting here for hours and no one will help me. I'm so thirsty, hungry, and tired!

SAM GOOD (still cautious, stands close, but out of reach of the blind man): I'm Sam Good. How did you happen to get to this bench?

MR. DELANEY: I came in on the 6 A.M. bus. Thought I was in Centerville, so I got off the bus. Then I discovered I wasn't at the usual stop. I walked until my cane hit the bench. I've been sitting here most of the day.

SAM GOOD: But it's 6:30 P.M. You've been sitting here all that time?

MR. DELANEY: Yes. I begged for someone to help me. I asked them to call the police, but no one would even talk to me. Am I in Centerville?

SAM GOOD: No, you're in Springfield. There's a restaurant down the street. I'll take you there and get you something to eat and drink.

*(He helps* MR. DELANEY *to his feet and they walk offstage together.)*

## Scene 2

(SAM GOOD *and* MR. DELANEY *are seated at a table in the restaurant.* MR. DELANEY *is eating.)*

SAM GOOD: Why are you traveling alone?

MR. DELANEY: I've come to Centerville quite frequently, and always got off at the right stop. My friend always met me at the bus station. When he wasn't there I knew I was at the wrong stop. He will be worried. *(Reaches into his pocket and pulls out several bills.)* Would you be so kind as to take this money, pay for the food and also call my friend and tell him that I'm OK? Here's his name and phone number.

(SAM GOOD *goes offstage for a few minutes, then returns.)*

SAM GOOD: Your friend was worried. He said when you didn't show up at the but stop, he called the apartment manager to learn if you had left. When he learned you left at six this morning, he called every place he could think of. I told him that I would drive you home.

MR. DELANEY: Thank you. You've restored my faith in the human race. This day has been a nightmare. I've never had such an experience. All those people passing by and not one of them would help a blind man.

SAM GOOD: Well, Mr. Delaney, people are just so afraid because so many terrible crimes have been committed lately. Just the other day a young man was killed when he went to the aid of a young woman who was being assaulted. Another case last week resulted in the beating and robbery of a man who went to help what he thought was a stranded motorist.

MR. DELANEY: But couldn't they see that I'm blind. What could a blind man do?

SAM GOOD: Unfortunately a criminal could put on dark glasses and carry a white cane. It's been done. People just don't know who to trust.

MR. DELANEY: Yes, the world is becoming rather frightening.

SAM GOOD: Actually you were fortunate not to have been harmed. Not long ago a blind man was beaten and robbed in this town. Perhaps you shouldn't travel unescorted.

MR. DELANEY: I always have the Lord with me. I knew He would send a ministering angel. M-m-m. You say your name is Sam Good? How appropriate. You are a Good Samaritan.

# The Joy of Discovery

**by Dorothy M. Brubaker**

**Characters:**

CHARLOTTE
ELEANOR
(CHARLOTTE *is sitting on porch reading.)*

## Scene 1

ELEANOR *(enters):* Look at the lady of leisure reading on a Monday morning. What is so interesting?

CHARLOTTE: The Bible.

ELEANOR: The Bible? Sounds frightfully dull. Give me something modern.

CHARLOTTE: Speaking of something modern. You probably think that women construction workers are very modern.

ELEANOR: Of course they are. Why, whoever heard of women construction workers until recently?

CHARLOTTE: The truth is, it's ancient, according to the Bible. I've been reading Nehemiah 3:12 about rebuilding the wall of Jerusalem. "And next unto him repaired Shallum the son of Halohesh, the ruler of the half part of Jerusalem, he and his daughters." And in 1 Chronicles 7:24, "And his daughter was Sherah, who built Beth-hor′-on the nether, and the upper, and Uz′-zen-she′-rah."

ELEANOR: How interesting. I want to remember that. *(Takes pencil and pad from table and writes.)* I just adore love stories. There are no love stories in the Bible.

CHARLOTTE: Oh yes there are! Why don't you start with Genesis 29—30? One of the most beautiful love stories in the Bible is the story of Jacob and Rachel. And the story of David and Bathsheba is in 2 Samuel 11.

ELEANOR: Seems I remember something about that one. Wasn't it about adultery?

CHARLOTTE: Yes, the Bible tells all. It doesn't whitewash the evil. But we learn lessons from their mistakes.

ELEANOR *(busy writing):* I don't suppose there are any outer space encounters?

CHARLOTTE: The original outer space encounters are in the Bible. A good place to start is Genesis 16—25.

ELEANOR: I'm going home and start reading. That is, if I can find a Bible. We did have one, but I'll have to hunt for it.

CHARLOTTE: I have several. Here, take this one.

ELEANOR *(takes Bible):* Thanks, Charlotte.

*(Interlude for group singing of "The B-I-B-L-E" or similar song)*

## Scene 2

*(*CHARLOTTE'S *patio,* CHARLOTTE *is watering plants.)*

ELEANOR *(enters, speaks excitedly):* Oh, Charlotte! You were right. The Bible is fabulous. I have been reading it to Tom and we've joined a Bible study group at our church. We are also attending Sunday night services. I found our Bible and it will always be used from now on.

CHARLOTTE: This is an answer to prayer!

ELEANOR: What do you mean?

CHARLOTTE: I've been praying that you and Tom would come to the Lord. Have you accepted Jesus as your Lord and Savior?

ELEANOR: Yes we have. Pastor led us to the Lord after prayer meeting!

---

## On the Defensive

How come we never react to preaching
Nor feel any stirrings within;
And then get all upset when the pastor
Begins to talk about sin?

*—Ruth M. Walsh*

# Inner Thoughts

**by Bill Bodell**

A fun and thought-provoking skit to be presented by senior adults—for their own enjoyment or for the enjoyment of others.

**Characters:**

*(First names depend on whether a man or woman assumes the role.)*

ROBERT/RITA READER
NANCY KNITTER
TOBY/TESSIE TALKER
WALDO/WINNIE WATCHER

READER sits farthest from exit. He/she is an uppity person who sits with a book in front of his face at opening.

KNITTER is preoccupied. Stares down at knitting or out over audience's head.

TALKER is a jolly person who is always ready to launch into a story—if someone will listen.

WATCHER is closest to the exit. He/she is temporarily hidden by the large TV set.

Note: For ease of playing, all four speak in the same order throughout. Scripts may be concealed in READER'S book, KNITTER'S knitting, TALKER'S lap, and WATCHER'S TV screen. All are seated as play begins.

**Setting**

Four chairs—spaced across playing area, facing audience
TV console—or large box with antenna. Person must be able to hide behind it.
Large book—or two pieces of cardboard approximately 9″ x 14″
Lecturn or music stand

READER *(loudly):* Well, I'll bet most people don't know that!

KNITTER: Most people don't know what?

READER: See, that proves my point. You should read a book sometime.

TALKER *(smiling)*: I read a book once. *(Thoughtfully)* At least, I *think* I did. That reminds me of the library in my old home town. Did I ever tell you about . . .

READER: It's *our* home town, too. And you've told us many times.

KNITTER: Many, *many* times.

*(If piano is available, the following may be sung or spoken to the tune of "Chopsticks.")*

READER: It doesn't matter, he just likes to chatter.
So listen, or don't as you please.

KNITTER: Telling a story puts him in his glory,
So tell me, how can we refuse?

TALKER: I am not bookish and not a bit hookish
I'm happiest when I can chat.

WATCHER *(from behind TV)*: Please all be quiet. Go back to your diet.
Of flipping and clicking and that! *(Song ends)*

*(Pushes TV to one side after finishing)*

READER: Surprise! Surprise! What brings you out of hiding?

KNITTER: Probably a commercial.

TALKER: Or a news update.

WATCHER *(triumphantly)*: Ah hah! None of the above. Haven't any of you noticed the time?

READER: Of course. It must be three o'clock.

KNITTER: How on earth did you know that?

TALKER: The soap operas end at three.

WATCHER: Don't call them that. They're nice little stories.

READER *(smugly)*: Not from what I've seen.

KNITTER: I'd rather sit here knitting and imagine all sorts of things.

TALKER: But reading and day dreaming and watching TV is no fun. They're all made up. I like to talk about the good old days.

WATCHER: See what I mean? He prefers fiction, too.

READER: All books aren't stories, you know. Lots of them are nonfiction. That's *real.*

KNITTER *(holds up knitting)*: And *this* is certainly real.

TALKER: Well, *some* of the things I talk about are real.

WATCHER: And so are some of the documentaries I watch on educational TV. *(Points at* READER) Poor soul must be lonely. He's always reading a book.

READER *(stands in place or at the lecturn to express inner thoughts. Others appear not to notice):*

One pet peeve, dear friends,
  I cannot overlook:
"He must be lonesome,
  He's reading a book."
They bother me daily,
  The Joans and the Herbs,
Distracting my nouns
  And transitive verbs.
I try not to notice
  Their stares and their gazes
While I'm joyfully lost
  In subjunctive phrases
The books I enjoy
  Have heroes grown taller
There's only one problem:
  The print's growing smaller.
By stretching and squinting
  At each page as it passes,
I put off the day when
  I'll have to buy glasses.
Ah, once I could handle
  The fine print of *Ben Hur*
But those times are changing
  Now it's only a blur.
If I sneak away now
  And find me a hovel,
Perhaps I'll be able
  To finish this novel!

*(Sits down and resumes reading)*

KNITTER *(to* WATCHER): She didn't hear you. She's lost somewhere between the covers of that book.

TALKER: Wonder what's for supper tonight? Hope it's not meat. They don't grow beef as tender as they used to.

WATCHER: Julia Child had a marvelous recipe on her show yesterday. Maybe I should send away for it.

READER *(pushes book out to arm's length):* May have to get glasses one of these days.

KNITTER *(stands in place or at the lecturn to express inner thoughts. Others appear not to notice):*

I first made a sweater
  But I did it all wrong.

One arm was too tiny
    And the other too long.
Now it did not matter
    To the wearer, poor soul,
Who tried hard but could not
    Push his head through the hole.
Then God taught me patience
    And the Book taught me more.
Now I sell my sweaters
    Straight away to the store.
The money they pay me
    Would fill up a barn!
Some goes to the Lord
    And the rest to buy yarn.
So when I just sit here
    As still as a kitten,
I'm really quite happy
    To stick to my knittin'!

*(Sits down and resumes knitting.)*

TALKER *(looks around at the others):* Say, did I ever tell you folks about . . .

OTHERS *(loudly and in unison):* Probably!

WATCHER: It's after four. Wonder what's on television?

READER: Oh, my goodness! *(Closes the book)*

KNITTER *(looks at* READER*):* What's the matter?

READER: I didn't expect it to end like that. After 500 pages.

KNITTER: You could have read the first chapter and then the last. *(Resumes knitting)* Would have saved you a lot of time.

TALKER *(stands in place or at the lectern to express inner thoughts. Others appear not to notice):*

I am just a reg'lar feller
And I'm quite a storyteller,
Specially tales of days gone by
That make you laugh or make you cry.
Of escapades when I was young
And quite a hero, though unsung.
With dashing deeds upon the field
No man or woman made me yield.
Yes, I can tell you, time and place
Where first I saw your smiling face.
But if you wore a constant frown,
I'd prob'ly never mark you down.
For those whose glass is halfway filled;
Whose life's a pickle, halfway dilled;
Whose sour pusses sadly sing;
No joy to life they ever bring.

I try to cheer them up at times
With tales of joy and lots of rhymes.
And they look at me, half believing—
It's entertainment! Not deceiving!
My glass is filled. I love to chat.
My tales are tall: I'll grant you that.
Don't believe *all* I say of me.
I exaggerate a bit, you see.
So if you've heard this tale before,
Have patience with this ancient bore.
There's one thing that will save the day.
*I* liked this story, anyway.

*(Sits down and looks around)* I wonder what's for supper tonight?

WATCHER: You hungry again? When I get that recipe, I'll let you read it.

READER: It's a shame you don't have it now. I'm completely out of reading material.

KNITTER: You can go read the embroidered plaques in my room.

TALKER: Or read the TV commercials with the sound turned off.

WATCHER *(stand in place or at the lecturn to express inner thoughts. Others appear not to notice):*

My favorite program, "Joys of Life,"
Is daily filled with tears and strife.
The heroine struggles to be free.
It could be worse; it could be *me.*
Often, I think I'm not too smart.
To follow the action takes a chart.
Rosie loves George . . . or is it Bob?
Keeping them straight is quite a job.
And Laura Lou's a real coquette.
Poor Rodney wishes they'd never met.
Amnesia struck him before, you see.
It should strike him again, it seems to me.
Sam has been killed: alas, alack.
Bill is missing. Jane wants him back.
Ann will marry in a big rush.
That whole story line makes me blush.
Sandra's deserted, poor little thing.
June is home now, after her fling.
Rose is screaming, chased by a knife.
That's the *good* parts of "Joys of Life"!

*(Returns to her chair, looks back at the others, shakes her head and exits)*

READER *(lays book on floor):* She's a strange one, all right. In all these years I've never figured her out.

KNITTER *(puts down knitting):* You'd think the people in her soap operas were real.

TALKER: I sneak a glance once in a while. Wasn't that way when I was young. *(Stands)* Think I'll go see what's for supper. *(Turns back)* Did I . . . ? *(Thinks better of it and exits)*

READER: I wonder which story he'll be telling us tonight?

KNITTER: Take your choice. We know them all by heart. *(Stands up)* I'll finish my sweater later. *(Exits)*

READER *(looks after the departed* KNITTER, *then around the empty stage):* I'll put the cover back on this book before it gets stepped on. *(Picks up book, carries it to stage left, placing it in imaginary bookcase)* What should I read next? *(Walks to center stage)* I'll bet I could write *my own book.* About these crazy brothers and sisters of mine. *(Walks to exit and pauses)* If only I knew their inner thoughts and more about them. Oh, well . . . *(Exits)*

---

## The Widow's Gift

(Mark 12:41-44)

The widow, who was giving but a pittance,
  The widow, who was giving all she had;
That widow did not know Christ spoke about her.
  (She would have been embarrassed, shy, and sad.)

She gave and went outside the temple gateway;
  She went to work, perhaps to sew or glean,
Perhaps to share her meager meal with someone;
  She lived from day to day in dull routine.

The widow went about her daily duties,
  Perhaps she gave again (Christ did not say);
She did not dream that she would be remembered,
  Yet, we recall her gift of love today.

*—Marjorie Stump*

## A Senior Adult's Adaptation of Psalm 118:24

**by Audre Pitts**

This is the day which the Lord hath made,
I will rejoice and be glad.
Whether in sunshine or whether in shade,
I will rejoice and be glad.

When I lose the hair off the top of my head,
I will rejoice and be glad.
When the cat has kittens on the spare-room bed,
I will rejoice and be glad.

When the well goes dry and the dog has fleas,
I will rejoice and be glad.
When I have the toothache in my knees,
I will rejoice and be glad.

When prices go up and my income down,
I will rejoice and be glad.
When a tire goes flat on the way to town,
I will rejoice and be glad.

When I fail no matter how hard I've tried,
I will rejoice and be glad.
When the parson's preaching gets under my hide,
I will rejoice and be glad.

When I can *hear* my arteries hardening,
I will rejoice and be glad.
When all my muscles are sore from gardening,
I will rejoice and be glad.

When I can't do my work, even though I try it,
I will rejoice and be glad.
When I keep falling off my diet,
I will rejoice and be glad.

When I simply can't remember names,
I will rejoice and be glad.
When I feel too old for playing games,
I will rejoice and be glad.

When my teeth fall out and I can't chew;
I will rejoice and be glad.
When I wear a hole in the sole of my shoe,
I will rejoice and be glad.

When I develop a hearing loss,
I will rejoice and be glad.
When my wife keeps trying to be the boss,
I will rejoice and be glad.

When I get soaked on a rainy day,
I will rejoice and be glad.
When a strong wind blows my wig away,
I will rejoice and be glad.

When people hint that I'm getting old,
I will rejoice and be glad.
When my husband's feet are always cold,
I will rejoice and be glad.

When I'm in a hurry and the bus is late,
I will rejoice and be glad.
When someone says, "Haven't you put on weight?"
I will rejoice and be glad.

When I wake up feeling dizzy,
I will rejoice and be glad.
When my hair is frazzled and frizzy,
I will rejoice and be glad.

When I'm not feeling fit as a fiddle,
I will rejoice and be glad.

When I start getting paunchy around
the middle,
I will rejoice and be glad.

When I feel worse than I've ever felt,
I will rejoice and be glad.
When my *knees* buckle, but not my
*belt,*
I will rejoice and be glad.

When the telephone interrupts my
snooze
I will rejoice and be glad.
When I can't bend over to tie my
shoes,
I will rejoice and be glad.

When I'm feeling down on my luck,
I will rejoice and be glad.
When I look in the mirror and it
says "Yuk!"
I will rejoice and be glad.

When I can't get the rockers going
on my chair,
I will rejoice and be glad.
When I sink my teeth in a steak, and
they *stay* there,
I will rejoice and be glad.

When I'm helped across the street by
a Boy Scout,
I will rejoice and be glad.
When just dialing long distance
wears me out,
I will rejoice and be glad.

When my shoulders begin to sag,
I will rejoice and be glad.
When my feet begin to drag,
I will rejoice and be glad.

When my steps are beginning to
slow,
I will rejoice and be glad.
When my mind says yes but my body
says no,
I will rejoice and be glad.

When I get to bed later than I wish,
I will rejoice and be glad.
When my false teeth grin at me from
their dish,
I will rejoice and be glad.

I am so tired I really can't think,
But I'll still rejoice and be glad.
My ball-point pen just ran out of ink,
So let's *all* rejoice and be glad!

---

## A Warm Love

**by Arthur H. Vaupel**

I had a critical illness not long ago,
Which made me fearful, as one might know.
But then I heard a whisper in my ear,
He said, "Fear thou not, for I am here."
Then I overcame my fear, just knowing
That God was near. Soon I was cured and all right,
But only through His grace and might.
Oh, what a comfort it is to have a love
From our Creator and Savior up above.
I'm thankful for the things of which
I've just written, as I can walk and see,
And I can breathe the air so free.
But there is really something else I need—
Just one more thing indeed; even though I try
To be a Christian to the letter,
I need to find a way to serve God better.

## Renewal

I bought it at a yard sale
At the very end of the day
When things were sorted over,
The rest to be given away.

It had a rocker missing
The cane was broken and old;
What once was a lovely finish
Was painted an ugly gold.

"Hard up for firewood, Lady?"
Someone teased as I dragged it away,
"Or do you need a broken prop
For a slum scene in a play?"

I heeded not their comments
For in my mind I could see,
With some work and loving attention,
Just what this piece could be.

Over the summer and into the fall,
I worked on it diligently.
A carpenter made a new rocker
But left the caning to me.

I sanded and scraped
And sanded some more,
While ugly gold paint chips
Fell to the floor.

At last the day came,
The sanding was done, a beautiful wood grain revealed.
Just a coat of stain to beautify
And several of varnish to keep it sealed.

No one would call it firewood now!
A gorgeous piece, a find!
Useful and ever so lovely,
Just like I'd seen in my mind!

And in the mind of God, a plan
Is in process for you and for me.
Something better than we know,
Something we someday can be.

Over the summer and into the fall
He works on us day and night,
And the Carpenter mends our broken lives
And holds us up to the light!

He sands and scraps our facades away
Until our true grain is revealed
And then He coats us with His love
And with His Spirit we're sealed

Sealed by His plan of redemption,
Perfected we'll one day be.
In the meantime, please be patient
For God isn't finished with me!

*—Priscilla J. Larson*

## It Isn't So Bad

I'm so very glad I'm nearing 80.
I've survived a lot of grief and strife.
Rearing one's children tries one's patience;
Now, I can enjoy the rest of life.

I once feared I'd lose my independence.
Being older, sometimes is profound.
True, I'm not as active as I used to be
But I thank the Lord my mind is sound.

Now I have more time to count my blessings,
Hours to read God's Word, to think and pray,
Time to see the beauty of a wrinkled face,
And to help a child along his way.

Though I know I'm pushing toward 100,
What delight to hear somebody say
That I really "don't look more than 60"
And I'm getting younger day by day!"

*—Lillian Pittman*

## Satisfaction

Satisfaction looms heavy o'er our
lives
And for this reason, everyone strives
To leap each hurdle with success
And thus ensure their happiness.
But what if time is not so fair?
It's more than many minds can bear.
Ambition's left to slip away,
Withdrawn—the heart has little to
say;
But faith in God's endless out
That too few people know about.
So when progress seems dim, meager,
and painstaking,
Reach out for His help—it's ours for
the taking.

*—Gary Ward*

## Fishing Makes a Man—a Boy Again

Awakening call of sunrise:
chirping birds, and whispering pines;
tangy smell of bacon, sputtering in a
pan;
early morning sounds, in clear moun-
tain air.
Fishing makes a man—a boy again.

Sparkling flash of fin, in a bubbling
brook;
flick of a rod, whirring of reel and
line;
the dart of a trout, at a brightly col-
ored fly;
a fighting battle, 'till landing the
prize.
Fishing makes a man—a boy again.

Setting of the sun, at end of day;
joy of proud accomplishment, as
homeward bound;
around the evening campfire, con-
tended peace;
for heaven and earth, God's love cre-
ated.
Fishing makes a man—a boy again.

*—Donna M. Schade*

## An Ode to Longevity of Life

Someone said,
"How old are you, Mac?
No kidding now,
just give me the facts."
So I came right out
and gave him the score;
I said, "It's none of your business;
I'm only 84."

I said to myself,
Maybe there's something to it.
I'll look in the glass
though I hated to do it.
I took one glance
and what did I see?
Something had happened
to this physiognomy.

My chin had moved up
and my nose had moved down.
My ears were both there
but I could hear nary a sound.
Now, hearing aids, glasses,
and teeth save the day;
And I'll fix my bald head
with a handsome toupee.

My eyes had sunk in,
I could hardly believe it.
Looked sorta like two
burnt holes in a blanket.
Well, I won't worry
cuz I still can see,
And a new pair'll be mine
when I reach eternity.

It matters not
what people say,
For I'm just living
from day to day.
And the good Lord reminds me,
"Harry, don't fret,
For what you saw in the glass
you'll soon forget!"

*—Harry McElrath*

## Sometimes

Sometimes
I'm knee-deep in glory
Surrounded by beauty
Running so lightly
at an effortless pace.
I'm passing through
a verdant valley
My eyes upon His face.

Sometimes
I aweary stumble
through dreary wilderness
Lifting leaden feet
Shuffling in the dust.
I'm climbing up
a desert mountain—
He's teaching me to trust.

*—Elaine Hart*

## The Closet of My Mind

I cleaned out the closet of my
mind
There was clutter in the corners
And dust on the shelf
There were memories tucked out
of sight
The things that made myself.

When all was swept
And all was scrubbed
And all was seen anew
I marveled at the gems I found
And wondered how they grew.

For You my God had taken
All the pieces of my life
You polished and You cut them
And wielded a sharp knife.

A crown sat waiting for me
With stones so neatly set
The rubies were my sorrows
And the trials I often met.

The sapphires my acceptance
Of the path You'd set for me
The emeralds were the beauty
Of the world You let me see.

The diamonds were my lifelong
tears
The happiness, the pains
The joy and the despair I bore
The sunshine and the rains.

My life is now a treasure
Before me to review
A precious crown of merit
My God, how I thank You!

*—Mary S. Ward*

## All His

I am His hands.
His tasks need mine to do them.
Mine are His legs
To hurry through the day.
My thoughts are His
To speak or keep in silence.
My ears to hear
His message: Peace! Be still.
My mind to know
The time to talk or listen.
My heart to beat
With love or sympathy.
My soul is filled
With His pure light and beauty,
For He's in me
And I live in His grace.

*—Esther B. Glaser*

## Isn't It Good to Know?

Isn't it good to know
when all days seem endless and
all hours are filled with pain and
all future has no meaning and
all dreams are in vain;
Isn't it good to know
when all paths are rough and
we stumble, fall, cry, and
all life passes by and
we have no place to go;
Isn't it good to know
that God is there beside us
reaching out with everlasting arms?
Isn't it good to know?

*—Helen Kitchell Evans*

# How High Is Your IQ?

### by Audre Pitts

I'm not speaking of your intelligence quotient,
I'm speaking of your I quit rating.
You might like to check yourself against these.

1. I quit teaching a Sunday School class because children make me nervous. (It really is nerve-racking when a first grader comes up with some scientific or electronic information of which I've never heard.)

2. I quit going to Sunday School as soon as my children were grown. Now I wait and come for church.

3. I quit singing in the choir a long time ago. I enjoy hearing *other* people sing.

4. I quit calling on people when I retired, now I expect others to call on me.

5. I quit tithing when I had to start living on my Social Security check. I don't think the Lord expects me to. (Are you *real sure* He doesn't?)

6. I quit going to prayer meeting on Wednesday evenings. After all, I'm not getting any younger and I get so tired by church time—especially after shopping all day.

7. I quit attending Sunday evening service because the music is geared to young people. It just isn't my type—and it's too loud.

8. I quit trying to memorize scripture. My memory is so poor now.

9. I quit shaking hands and greeting people after services because I get *so embarrassed* when I can't remember their names. (Try saying Hi or Hello and maybe they won't even know you have a problem.)

10. I quit sending notes and greeting cards to our shut-ins when postage got so high. After all, __ cents is a lot to spend on a stamp. I have to watch my money now that I am retired.

11. I quit being friendly toward children and teenagers. What do they care about an oldster like me?

12. I quit praying with seekers at the altar because of my arthritis. (Don't laugh if you've never had it!)

13. I quit going to the pastor when I have a big problem. Why should he waste valuable time on someone my age? He should be helping the younger ones.

14. I quit volunteering to help with cleanup work at church. Let the youngers ones do it.

15. I quit helping in the nursery. I raised my own children and that's enough.

16. I quit going to funerals and memorial services because I don't like to think about dying.

17. I quit associating closely with some of the elderly in our church. I'm afraid people will think I'm as old as they are.

18. I quit going to church potlucks because I hate to cook, now that I'm alone.

19. I quit visiting in nursing homes because I don't want to think of myself being in one someday—maybe.

20. I quit trying to be cheerful when I have aches and pains. After all these years, don't I deserve a little sympathy?

I hope you come out with a very low I quit score. I had to say "ouch" once in a while, myself, as I wrote this.

---

## No First Person Singular?

The Lord gave us a prayer
   To use every day.
"Our Father which art in heaven"
   And thus we often pray.

But we can't say His prayer
   And even once say "I,"
Nor can we repeat it
   And use the word "my."

You'll note everything is "our,"
   In this meaningful plea:
It's "our" Father or give "us."
   But not one *me!*

*—Ruth M. Walsh*

# S.A.L.T.* Dinner/Party

*(*Senior Adults Living Triumphantly)*

**by Zeta Combs Davidson**

Here is a senior adult activity that can take the form of a dinner or a party. Its theme is based upon the New Testament concept that Christians are salt in their world. Use it to launch a senior adult fellowship organization.

### Invitation

Invite all senior adults in the church to a special dinner or party. Instruct each to bring his own salt in a special container: a shaker, box, or whatever.

### Decorations

Make posters that bear familiar thoughts about salt:

"Not worth his salt"
"Pass the salt, please"
"You are the salt of the earth"
"When it rains, it pours"
etc.

Table decorations may include collections of salt and pepper shakers; blocks of livestock salt; boxes of Morton's salt, grouped with Bibles opened to Matthew 5:13. The passage should be indicated by a brightly colored arrow cut from construction paper.

### As Guests Gather

In various areas around the room, position displays that show how salt is used.

Person soaking cucumbers in brine
Cranking old-fashioned ice-cream freezer using rock salt
Making french fries
Popping porcorn with big salt shaker nearby

Have food samples at each display.

### The Dinner

Serve a meal that most people will enjoy. However, whatever the menu, omit salt from the food preparation. Each person will salt to taste from his own personal salt shaker.

**Program**

After dinner the following dialogue may be presented. Throughout the evening, the master of ceremonies will serve as M.C. for all activities. The program may be used to launch S.A.L.T. as a senior adult organization. If such an organization is not to be established, the program may end with spontaneous testimonies based on another's "saltiness" having been an influence, or how one has striven to be "salt" in a given situation.

MASTER OF CEREMONIES: No one has to guess that salt can make the difference in the world. We have been seeking a name for this delightful group. We want it to be easily understood. We want it to describe who we are. We want it to state our purpose. We propose to the group that we, from this time forward, be known as S.A.L.T. (Do not reveal what the letters S.A.L.T. stand for as yet.)

READER NO. 1: Salt is known to all mankind. Salt is probably the oldest preservative and seasoning. Salt is a basic chemical. Salt is so necessary to the functioning of the body that life cannot go on without it. Salt is needed in many different sizes, shapes, and types to meet the special requirements of today's industries. Salt definitely has purpose in the life of the world.

*(In the following part of the program each of these purposes of salt will be restated by the* READER. *Another* READER *will respond appropriately after each purpose is restated.)*

READER NO. 1: Salt is known to all mankind.

READER NO. 2: Most of us here have been Christians for a long time. We have watched the life of this church in many situations. *(Relate one or two to personalize the program)* Yes, because we are known to just about everybody in this church and are vital participants as church members, we qualify . . .

READER NO. 1: Salt is probably the oldest preservative and seasoning.

READER NO. 2: Bacteria cannot live in a salty environment. We want to preserve the right spirit in our church by leading lives in which the bacteria of sin cannot exist.

READER NO. 1: "Pass the salt"—It's a universal seasoning agent.

READER NO. 2: No matter what the meal, salt is important to make food tastier. As S.A.L.T., we will strive to sprinkle ourselves throughout the organizations of this church to produce tasty nourishment as others satisfy their hunger for God's Word.

READER NO. 1: Salt is a basic chemical. It is used in the production of many other chemicals. The chemicals made from salt are important in manufacturing paper, soap, leather, glass, fertilizer, textile dyes, explosives, and a host of other items.

READER NO. 2: As S.A.L.T., we are willing to be used in the production of growing Christians within our church family. We recognize our responsibility to play an important part in the basic instruction of others so that God may use them for His purpose.

READER NO. 1: Salt is necessary to the functioning of the body. Life cannot go on without it. Without salt, the fluids of the body cannot be kept in proper balance.

READER NO. 2: As S.A.L.T., we recognize our purpose in the life of the Body of Christ—the Church. We will continue in Bible study and prayer so that we may actively know our function in the body.

READER NO. 1: Salt is needed in many different sizes, shapes, and types to meet all the special requirements of today's industries. *Fine*-grained salt is needed for cake mixes. *Pure* salt is needed for butter. *Rock* salt is needed for melting ice. Salt *blocks* are needed for livestock. We could go on.

READER NO. 2: As S.A.L.T., we have the experience necessary to serve. We could say that we come in all sizes, shapes, and types, but we prefer to suggest that each of us is unique. We can make special contributions to meet the special needs of today's church.

READER NO. 1: Salt makes people thirsty.

READER NO. 2: As S.A.L.T., we will continue to live Christian lives that will point others toward righteous living. We know that "blessed are those who . . . thirst after righteousness." We also know that salt can irritate; we know that *too much* salt makes a brine that is extremely distasteful. We want to produce only thirst.

READER NO. 1: Salt has a purpose in the life of the world. The value of salt has long been known in history. All of us have known someone "not worth his salt." Long ago, salt was used for wages—hence we really could say, we work for a *sal*-ary.

READER NO. 2: We want to function in the world as God leads us. We know something of our value—even though we are as common as salt—we can make the difference.

MASTER OF CEREMONIES: We are S.A.L.T. *(Unfurl a banner that reads* **S** *enior* **A** *dults* **L** *iving* **T** *riumphantly.)*

Note: If the dinner is not for establishing a S.A.L.T. organization, the M.C. may ask for testimonials from those who have been salt in a particular situation or have come in contact with one who has been salt to them.

# Historical Banquet Skit

*Unannounced, Spontaneous Event*

**by Cynthia S. Baker**

*(Playing time: Approximately 20 minutes)*

**Production Notes:**

The play is written to be put on in a dining room after a dinner has been served in connection with a historical celebration for the church, such as a centennial, sesquicentennial, or bicentennial event. It is intended that, when the play begins, none of the people perceive right away that it *is* a play. Therefore, since the play is unannounced and unexpected, it has no title, and should not be announced ahead of time.

**Setting:**

A small cleared area in the room where the pastor can stand with his back to the entrance that the "oldtimers" can use. No scenery is required. However, a very beautiful, historic atmosphere can be created for the dining room by borrowing and hanging old quilts on the walls between the windows. Tables should have tablecloths, and be lighted either by kerosene lights or hurricane candles.

**Cast:**

OLDTIMERS will have costumes, and will appear through the door behind the pastor. MODERN VOICES should be church members planted here and there in the dining room, with nothing to call attention to them until they begin to speak. PASTOR'S role is critical, in making the people believe that what is taking place is simply an impromptu church meeting. Since he is in control of the "meeting," he can control the action by calling only on "planted" individuals.

OLDTIMER NO. 1 *(Bearded if possible; wearing coonskin cap, moccasins, dark trousers, ragged flannel shirt, and an arrow through his chest, with blood stains on shirt where arrow goes in and comes out. See directions below)*

OLDTIMER NO. 2 *(Woman with long sleeved, high necked, floor length dress; plain collar, full skirt; also ruffled "mobcap" and white apron)*

OLDTIMER NO. 3 *(Teenage boy, wearing blue coat, blue short pants, overlarge white collar, big bow tie)*

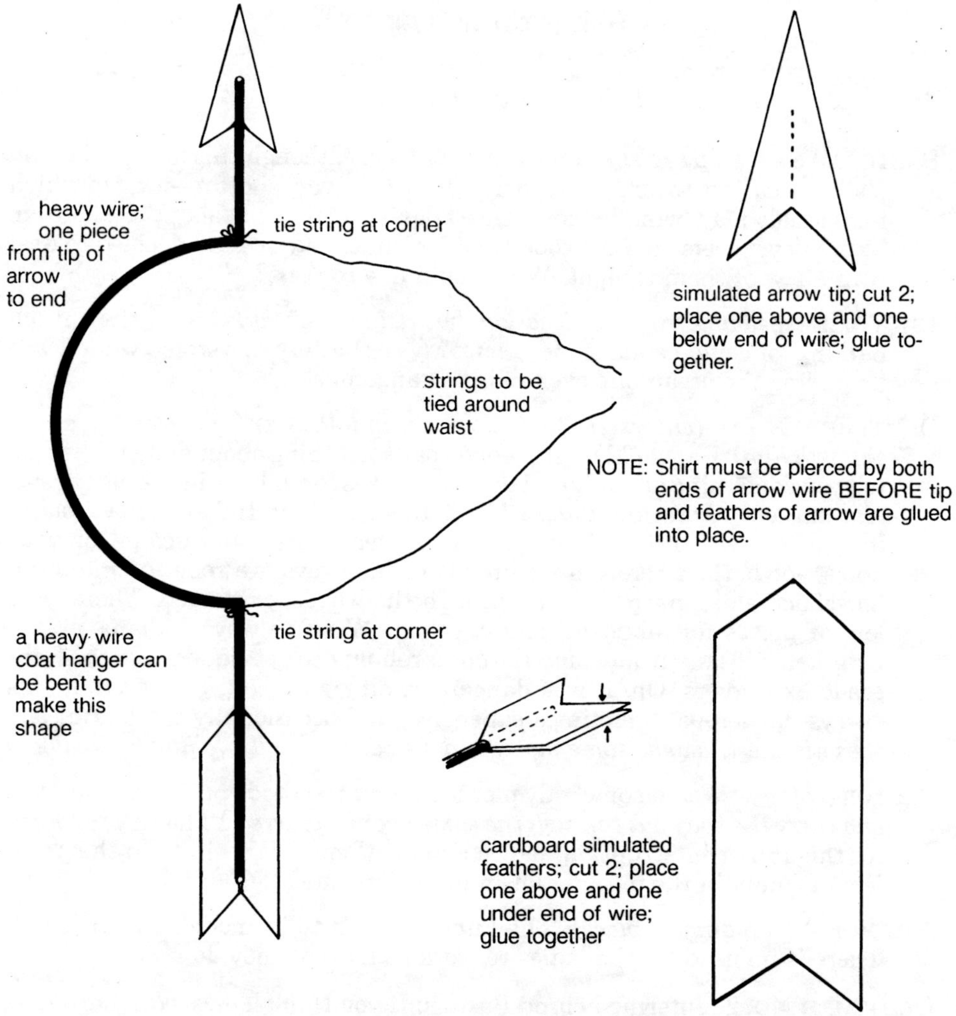


OLDTIMER NO. 4 *(Man wearing frock coat, ruffled white shirt, or clothing suited to the period)*

PASTOR *(Dressed in ordinary dinner clothes)*

1ST VOICE *(Church organist or pianist)*

2ND VOICE *(Woman involved in church kitchen ministry)*

3RD VOICE *(Sunday School boy or girl about 11)*

4TH VOICE *(Older man)*

**Script:**

The oldtimer speeches refer to specific historical events and customs and should be altered as necessary.

## **Skit** (following dinner)

*(Any opening remarks would be appreciated, such as introducing guests, etc. Ask people to turn their chairs toward you.)*

PASTOR: We are going to ask you to bear with us. Although this is a special and festive occasion, we are going to take time for a very short meeting in which individuals may bring up some miscellaneous concerns about the church. There never seems to be a good time for these, and we have decided to deal with a few of them tonight. Who would like to start?

1ST VOICE *(speaking from her location, but rising to speak):* I wish the church parking lot could be made more safe. My car battery was stolen while I was practicing the organ one evening! It's dangerous!

OLDTIMER NO. 1 *(enters through door behind* PASTOR, *staggering, arrow through him):* Danger? Did somebody say something about danger? Let me tell you something about how dangerous it was for us back in the early days. *(He staggers a little, and coughs.)* Now, this here is an Indian arrow *(coughing),* of course, and Indians were a problem. After your scalp—or your horse—or both. There were no roads or highways; we rode to church on horseback along narrow trails through the woods, or walked. There were lots of places for ambush. *(pause, cough)* Wasn't always Indians, either. Drunken ruffians from some flatboat, robbing to get liquor. *(cough)* Renegade ex-soldiers. Oh, it was dangerous, all right. *(cough, stagger)* It was always dangerous, sometimes expensive, and occasionally fatal. *(He clutches his chest, coughs some more, and dies dramatically, falling to the floor.)*

PASTOR *(calmly):* Would somebody please remove that body? *(Two people come and carry the body out through the same door he entered.)* Thank you. Sorry for this minor interruption, ladies and gentlemen. We will keep the problem of safety in the parking lot in mind. Anyone else?

2ND VOICE *(standing in place):* The kitchen needs to be made more efficient. There is no need for the ladies to work as hard as they do now.

OLDTIMER NO. 2 (entering behind Pastor): If you think ladies work hard now, let me tell you how hard it used to be—no big dining room like this, no kitchen at all, no electricity. We didn't even have running water or indoor plumbing. That didn't stop us from having church picnics and suppers. We carried water over in buckets and either brought food prepared at home or cooked it over open fires.

One time at a church picnic it started to rain, and we took the legs off the tables, carried the tops into the sanctuary, and laid the tabletops across the pews! *(She goes back out through the door.)*

PASTOR: Thank you. I'm sure the Construction Committee will be mindful of any constructive suggestions about the kitchen. Someone else. Yes?

3RD VOICE *(standing up):* I just want to say I'd like Sunday School better if we didn't have to memorize so much.

OLDTIMER NO. 3 *(coming in through door):* Did someone say something about memorizing? You should have come to Sabbath School with me! If you look at the old records, you'll see notations beside the names to show how many verses each had learned and recited. Now me, I learned the whole of Psalm 119—all 176 verses. I will recite it for you now:

> Blessed are the undefiled in the way, who walk in the law of the Lord. Blessed are they that keep his testimonies, and that seek him with the whole heart. They also . . .

PASTOR *(interrupting hastily):* Yes, thank you very much—

OLDTIMER NO. 3 *(continues as if he hasn't heard):* Thou has commanded us to keep . . .

PASTOR: Thank you again—

*(Enter two people who take* OLDTIMER NO. 3 *by both arms and lead him back out through the door. He continues to recite as he is led away.)*

OLDTIMER NO. 3: O that my ways were directed to keep thy statues! Then shall I not be ashamed, when I have respect unto all thy commandments. I will praise thee . . . *(exit)*

PASTOR: It certainly is a commendable display of effort to have memorized 176 verses. However, in the interests of time, we had better proceed. Any other concerns?

4TH VOICE *(rising):* How's the air-conditioning project coming along? It would be nice to have more comfort during the Sunday services.

OLDTIMER NO. 4 *(entering behind* PASTOR*):* You want to talk about comfort? Let me tell you how it used to be! Air-conditioning consisted of opening the door to the outside, and that meant an occasional dog or cat would stroll down the aisle. In the winter you roasted or froze, depending upon how far away you were from the potbellied wood stove in the aisle. Way, way back, they thought nothing of a four-hour service. It wasn't quite that bad in my day.

As a matter of fact, we had our own ideas of comfort. I notice you don't have any spittoons now. Things just aren't what they used to be! *(Exits, shaking his head.)*

PASTOR: Wait a minute, wait a minute—come back out here, all you Oldtimers. *(All four of them come back into the room.)* And you people who have spoken here today *(looking out over the congregation),* please stand up. *(They stand.)*

Now, you Oldtimers are talking about hardships. And you people here *(to the* VOICES*)* are talking about comfort. I don't say either one is wrong. But is that really the point? Is that the church you're talking about? Or just the building in which the Church meets? What was your purpose, Oldtimers? What was it all about?

OLDTIMER NO. 1: Why, we stood foursquare for the Word of God!

OLDTIMER NO. 2: We put our hands in God's hand, and we walked in faith.

OLDTIMER NO. 3: We learned the Word.

OLDTIMER NO. 4: We preached the Word, and taught the Word, and tried to obey the Word, and we did it in the teeth of the wilderness.

PASTOR *(turning to the others):* And what about us?

1ST VOICE: We stand on the Word of God, too. You've got nothing on us.

2ND VOICE: It still takes faith, and we walk in faith.

3RD VOICE: We learn the Word, too.

4TH VOICE: And we also preach the Word, and teach the Word, and do our best to obey the Word. And brother, the wilderness is still at the door! It may not be the same kind of wilderness, but it's there!

OLDTIMERS *(together):* We were the Church!

VOICES *(together):* We *are* the Church!

PASTOR: That's more like it! Jesus Christ is the same yesterday, and today, and forever. Let's all stand and close with a song that says that, and let's put our hearts into it—all of us!

**Closing Hymn:** "O God, Our Help in Ages Past" or "The Church's One Foundation"

*(If passing out books is disruptive, cue cards may be used.)*

---

## Good News—or Advice

Christianity began as the Good News;
For salvation, Christ paying the price.
But now it's too often diluted
Into just "good advice"!

*—Ruth M. Walsh*

# Valentine Fellowship

by Dorothy M. Brubaker

## Preparation

In advance, interview several members of the group who have been or are happily married. Answers may be written down or taped by interviewer. The information is then used to formulate situations for impromptu skits. These are typed on 3″ x 5″ cards. Ask the following questions:

Was there anything unusual, unique, humorous
(1) about how you met?
(2) about your courtship?
(3) about your wedding?
(4) about your honeymoon?
(5) about your first weeks of married life?

Each situation card is numbered, Skit No. 1, Skit No. 2, etc. The situation will be listed as follows:

Their Song: "One Alone"
Favorite Hymn: "Constantly Abiding"
Situation: Met at church skating party in Cleveland; dated while in high school. During depression, boy went to California to work; transferred back to Cleveland; went to restaurant for lunch, waitress was old girlfriend; started dating again; became engaged while on roller coaster.

Also prepare a large frame, wide enough to accommodate two persons standing side by side. Make it high enough for any six footers. *See Drawing A below:*

FRAME: *Drawing A*

The frame is covered with white paper or cloth. Cut out two heart-shaped openings; the highest one for male, shorter for female. Make a heart-shaped frame around these openings of cloth, paper, or paint in red. Attach a bow tie to the male frame, a ribbon bow to the female frame.

**Invitations**

*See Drawing B:*

You guys crank up the Lizzie,
  C'mon dress up, you gals,
Break out some old styles,
  And bring along some pals,
For a sentimental journey
  Down Memory Lane,
Let you and your honey
  Be valentines again.

DATE: __________ TIME: __________

PLACE: ____________________________

POTLUCK: Bring box lunch for one decorated as valentine. These will be auctioned in a "silent" auction.

*Drawing B*

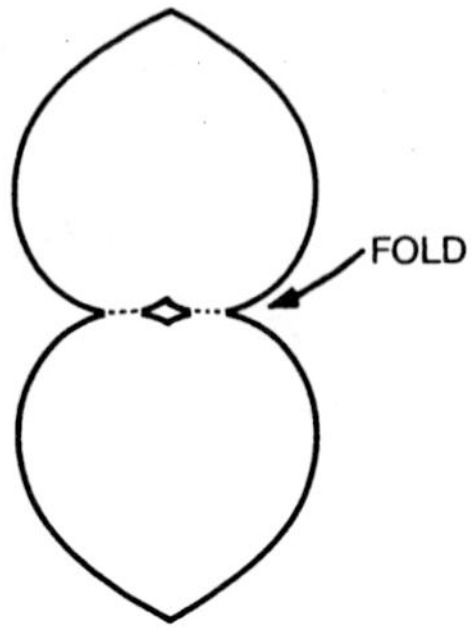


**Program**

As guests arrive they are given name tags *(See Drawing C),* and are instructed to place their "valentine" lunches on the auction table. As each lunch is placed on the table, a 3″ x 5″ blank card is attached to it. Guests may then start silent bidding. They write the amount of money they will pay and place their initials by it on the 3″ x 5″ bidding card. If someone else wants the same lunch, he will cross out the previous bid and write a higher bid and initial it. This silent bidding is open until time is called. In order to claim lunch, bidder must pay the amount he bid.

NAME TAGS:
*Drawing C*

Both invitations and name tags are made of red construction paper. Invitation has white insert for printing data. Name tag heart is glued to white lace paper doily.

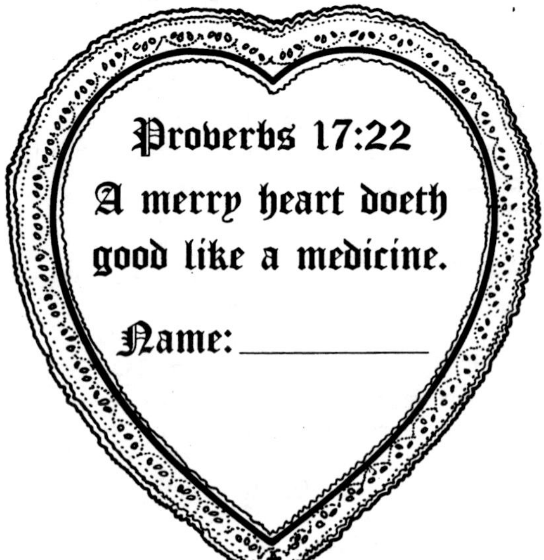

### Skits

After eating, guests are asked to check the number written on the back of their name tags. Every person will have a number. These numbers will depend on the number of skits used and the number in attendance. It is best to limit each group of numbers to four or five. Thus all those with number 1 will receive a situation card listed as Skit No. 1, etc.

Each group dramatize the situation listed on their skit card. The audience may guess whose story was dramatized. Then, as their song is being played, sung, etc., the real couple or individual appears in the picture frame.

The fellowship ends happily with group singing of old love songs familiar to their age-group.

---

## Immutable

Despite inflation,
  Or who's to blame,
The wages of sin
  Remain the same.

*—Ruth M. Walsh*

## Unknowingly

Ignorant of the fits we throw,
Wanton acts as sinners go,
Forging paths to what we'll reap.
Knowing not what tone to keep,
Where partial good's a mere elite
And endless good remains unique!
Shed the old, strap on the new.
Prepare ourselves through what we do.

*—Gary Ward*

## Why of the Word

Scripture is designed by God
  To give us information;
But, even more important than that
  It gives *transformation!*

*—Ruth M. Walsh*

*Director's Notes*